NARROW GAUGE
RAILWAYS
of
NORTH WALES

To Mum and Dad,
who first introduced me to the delights of the Welsh Narrow Gauge,
to Chris who has learnt to accept them
and to the volunteers who keep them running.

NARROW GAUGE
RAILWAYS
of
NORTH WALES

ANDREW WILSON

The
History
Press

Acknowledgements

I would like to thank all those people who have helped me with photographs: Paul Chancellor; Frank Hornby; Hugh Davies; Cliff Thomas; the Kidderminster Railway Museum and Desmond Coakham. Any errors are mine and mine alone.

First published in 2003 by Tempus Publishing Limited
Reprinted 2007

Reprinted in 2011 by
The History Press
The Mill, Brimscombe Port,
Stroud, Gloucestershire, GL5 2QG
www.thehistorypress.co.uk

Reprinted 2013

British Library Cataloguing in Publication Data.
A catalogue record for this book is available from the British Library.

ISBN 978 0 7524 2788 1

Typesetting and origination by Tempus Publishing Limited
Printed and bound in Great Britain by
Marston Book Services Limited, Didcot

Contents

Introduction

It was all of forty years ago, during the summer of 1963, that I came under the spell of the narrow gauge railways of North Wales. I suppose if anyone is blame for this it must be my mother, who scanned the pages of Dalton's weekly paper for an affordable self-catering cottage in Snowdonia. She found Dolorgan, a cottage in the hills above Talsarnau, near Harlech, that both met her requirements and opened the eyes of her son to the magical world of steam, mountains, hills, lakes and the sea, all of which so characterise this part of the world. Locomotives and places with seemingly unpronounceable names, that had previously only been two-dimensional monotone images on the pages of *Meccano Magazine*, *Trains Illustrated* and the *Railway Magazine*, suddenly became reality. I was well and truly hooked, so much so that the decline of steam on British railways seemed much less cataclysmic when set against the rich diversity and charm of the Welsh narrow gauge railways.

Four decades ago, driving from Fulham in south-west London, to Talsarnau, was not for the faint-hearted, especially when travelling via Worcester and Welshpool. When the car involved

The cottage that started it all, Dolorgan, high in the hills above Talsarnau.

WPA 172 outside Dolorgan in August 1963.

was a blue 1959 Ford 103E Popular, WPA 172, heavily laden with five passengers and a loaded roof rack, the journey began to take on epic proportions. Despite its 1172cc side valve engine, the three-speed gearbox, top speed of around 50mph and vacuum-operated windscreen wiper made long drives a test of the driver and passengers' endurance.

The first encounter with the Welsh narrow gauge came at Welshpool, where the rusty 2ft 6in tracks of the Welshpool & Llanfair Light Railway crossed Church Street before disappearing between houses and backyards to reappear at Raven Square, only to vanish once more into verdant, impenetrable vegetation. At Llanfair Caereinion a home signal marked the site of a bucolic terminus. Still travelling westward, the next encounter was rather more distant, with a plume of white steam marking the Fairbourne Railway across the Mawddach Estuary south of Barmouth. The two weeks spent at Dolorgan ended with the Festiniog and Snowdon Mountain railways having been discovered, as well as the trackbeds of the long-abandoned Corris and Welsh Highland railways.

The following August saw Dolorgan re-visited, this time in a beige Ford 105E Anglia, 686 EYW, with an 1198cc engine. The Anglia's improved performance and comfort made the 275-mile journey less tedious and time consuming, although father insisted on setting off in the middle of the night. Travelling north on the M1 and breakfasting by the side of the A5 near Brownhills, the journey was just the exciting precursor to further narrow gauge delights. This year the Talyllyn, Vale of Rheidol and Great Orme Tramway were added to the list of new discoveries. Although geographically not strictly in North Wales, I always think of the Vale of Rheidol and Welshpool & Llanfair railways as being part of the north. The vast quarries at Dinorwic, alongside Llyn Padarn, were also found, although off limits to the general public. By the time of our last visit to Dolorgan in 1971, all the narrow gauge railways north of Aberystwyth had been explored, including the newly opened Llanberis Lake Railway and what was to become the Bala Lake Railway.

One of the joys of the Welsh narrow gauge is its sheer variety and apparent antiquity. Most gauges varied between 15in and 2ft 7 ½ in with the majority settling for 1ft 11 ½ in or thereabouts. However, of the odd ones out, the 3ft 6in Great Orme Tramway survived while the 4ft Padarn Railway did not, although the Llanberis Lake Railway now uses part of the

686 EYW at Dolorgan in August 1964.

trackbed. Many of the railways were designed from the outset as miniature mainlines while others were constructed on a shoestring. A few were wholly industrial in origin whereas others were built to serve agricultural communities. Some were grandiose in concept while others reflected the needs of a local community. If the railways had anything in common it was their individuality and uniqueness.

However, those concerns still operating in the 'we've never had it so good' 1960s were very different organisations to the railways of the 1920s and 1930s. The Festiniog and Talyllyn had avoided being absorbed by either the Great Western or LMS in 1923 and had gone their own idiosyncratic ways, while the Corris, Vale of Rheidol and Welshpool & Llanfair had all come under the umbrella of Swindon. Somehow the independent Snowdon Mountain Railway, the Fairbourne, Glyn Valley and Great Orme Tramway were also left to plough their individual furrows in an increasingly road-orientated society. The wholly industrial railways that serviced the declining slate industry in North Wales were concentrated close to Snowdon at Dinorwic, Bethesda and Penrhyn and continued to do what they were best at: moving huge tonnages of slate from the quarries to the transhipment quays.

When I first discovered the Welshpool & Llanfair and Festiniog in 1963 the picture was dramatically different, as the socio-economic conditions of the post-war years conspired against such traditional forms of transport. Yet the first casualty had occurred three decades earlier when the Glyn Valley Railway's remaining freight services between Chirk and the quarries at Ceiriog were withdrawn in July 1935, only twenty-seven months after the last passenger train ran. The 1930s also saw the cessation of passenger services on the Corris Railway and the Welshpool & Llanfair Railway in 1931 and the complete closure of the uneconomic Welsh Highland Railway in 1937.

Despite the decline of the Welsh slate industry, the majority of Welsh narrow gauge railways struggled through the war years, either providing a very basic service or being moth-balled. Having continued to run slate trains on three days a week throughout the war, the Festiniog finally succumbed in August 1946 at the beginning of the Blaenau Ffestiniog quarry holidays. The next closure came in August 1948 when British Railways shut down the Corris Railway after flood waters had irrevocably damaged the Dovey Bridge near Machynlleth.

By the mid-1950s preservation societies had revived the fortunes of the Talyllyn and Festiniog railways. British Railways had continued where the Great Western had left off by continuing to promote and run the Vale of Rheidol as one of Aberystwyth's tourist attractions. The Snowdon Mountain Railway was continuing to do what it was built for, namely carrying tourists to the top of Snowdon, weather permitting. The Great Orme was likewise quietly plying its trade by carrying passengers from Llandudno to the top of the Great Orme. Further south, the Fairbourne Railway was maintaining its summer boat train service between the isolated village of Fairbourne and Penrhyn Point, on the southern banks of the Mawddach, where, in the shadow of Cader Idris, connections were made with the ferry to Barmouth.

Perhaps the most surprising survivor was British Railway's Welshpool & Llanfair branch, which maintained a basic goods service until 1956. Following the precedent of the Talyllyn and Festiniog railways, ownership of the line eventually passed to a preservation society.

Although the market for Welsh slate had contracted to the point that it was only a fraction of what it had been a century before, the 1950s and 1960s were to see it all but disappear completely. What slate was being quarried was more likely to be shipped out of Wales by road than by railway. By 1956 the Penrhyn Quarry Railway had lines of withdrawn and stored locomotives at Bethesda. At Blaenau Ffestiniog the quarries were still using hundreds of ex-Festiniog slate wagons but only as internal user wagons. Gradually the remaining industrial narrow gauge lines fell out of favour and use.

October 1961 saw the closure of the Padarn Railway. The Penrhyn Quarry Railway stopped working towards the end of the summer of 1962 and the Nantlle Railway ceased operations in 1963. The final closure came in November 1967 when the Dinorwic Quarries ceased operations.

Since the 1960s the Welsh narrow gauge scene has changed out of all recognition. Tourism has become a major industry in North Wales creating jobs, attracting visitors from all over the world and creating significant levels of income for local businesses. All the railways have responded by marketing themselves as prime attractions and many joined forces in 1970 to market themselves under the banner of 'The Great Little Trains of Wales'.

The ever innovative Festiniog Railway built the only spiral in Britain at Dduallt to allow it to re-open to Blaenau Ffestiniog. Not to be outdone, the Talyllyn Railway upgraded the line from Abergynolwyn to Nant Gwernol to carry passengers. The Welshpool & Llanfair has built a new terminal on the outskirts of Welshpool at Raven Square and British Railways finally rid itself of the Vale of Rheidol by selling it to the owners of the Brecon Mountain Railway.

Perhaps the most significant development has been the building of new narrow gauge railways aimed wholly at the tourist trade. The Llanberis Lake Railway was established on part of the trackbed of the Padarn Railway in 1971 and the following year the Bala Lake Railway opened to passengers along the shore of Lake Bala on the course of part of the ex-Great Western line from Dolgelly to Bala. The greatest of all the Welsh narrow gauge challenges, the re-opening of the Welsh Highland Railway has been started by the Festiniog Railway and the Welsh Highland (1964) Co. 2002 also saw the return of the Corris Railway as a passenger line with the running of trains between Corris and Maespoeth.

My intention in this book is to show how the Welsh narrow gauge railways have changed in the last half century and I make no excuses for the nostalgia that exudes from the following pages. The railways are arranged in the order in which I first discovered them in the 1960s.

Author's Note

In this book, the style used for the place names during the 1950s and 1960s period has been maintained, while for the post-1970 period current spellings are used.

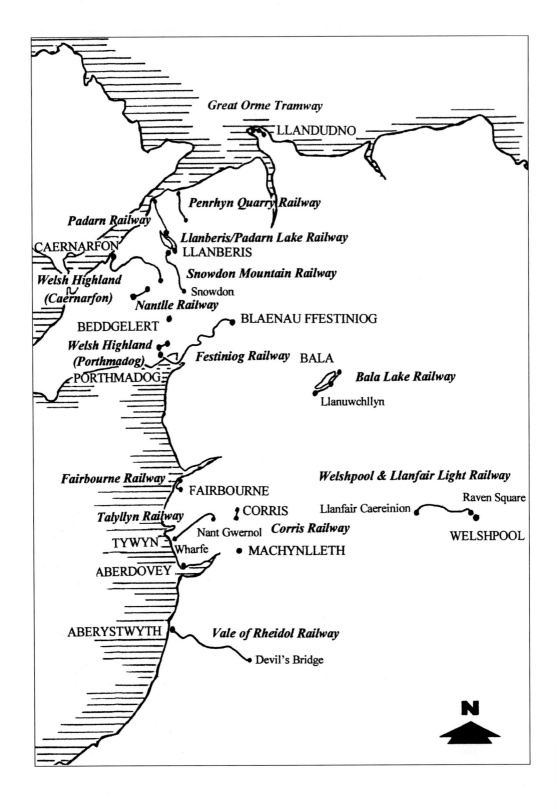

Great Orme Tramway

LLANDUDNO

Penrhyn Quarry Railway

Padarn Railway

Llanberis/Padarn Lake Railway

CAERNARFON

LLANBERIS

Snowdon Mountain Railway

Welsh Highland
(Caernarfon)

Snowdon

Nantlle Railway

BLAENAU FFESTINIOG

BEDDGELERT

Welsh Highland
(Porthmadog)

BALA

Festiniog Railway

Bala Lake Railway

PORTHMADOG

Llanuwchllyn

Welshpool & Llanfair Light Railway

Fairbourne Railway

FAIRBOURNE

Raven Square

Talyllyn Railway

CORRIS

Llanfair Caereinion

Nant Gwernol

Corris Railway

WELSHPOOL

TYWYN

Wharfe

MACHYNLLETH

ABERDOVEY

ABERYSTWYTH

Vale of Rheidol Railway

Devil's Bridge

N

One

Welshpool & Llanfair Light Railway

Conceived under the light railway legislation, the Welshpool & Llanfair Light Railway took two years to build and opened in 1903. Operated by the Cambrian Railways, passenger traffic was never particularly remunerative and ceased in 1931 under the auspices of the Great Western Railway (GWR). Goods traffic, however, remained buoyant, serving as it did the local farming communities until 1956.

Within a month of closure by British Railways a preservation society had been formed, but it was to be April 1963 before the railway was officially re-opened. The original Beyer Peacock 0-6-0Ts, The Earl and The Countess, returned to service, since when several additions have been made to the locomotive stock from Britain, Austria, Antigua, Sierra Leone and Finland. As the original passenger coaches had been scrapped by the GWR the new owners had to look elsewhere. As a result, coaches have been sourced from the Chattenden & Upnor Railway, the Zillertalbahn in Austria, Sierra Leone and Hungary.

Unlike other Welsh narrow gauge railways, the WLLR is not located in a major tourist area. However, it has continued to attract visitors and develop its facilities. A new station has been built at Raven Square, Welshpool and its presence next to the A458 helps keep it in the public eye.

On 6 April 1963 the Welshpool & Llanfair Light Railway officially re-opened, almost six and a half years after the last British Railways train ran on 3 November 1956. The first train, comprising a semi-open toastrack coach and the combination car, is seen threading its way between Church Street and Union Street behind The Earl. (Paul Chancellor Collection)

In June 1956 a special train made up of two brake vans and two open wagons was organised. Seating was provided in the open wagons by platform benches. No.822, named *The Earl* by the Cambrian Railways when delivered from Beyer Peacock in September 1902, is in charge of the special at the old passenger terminus in Welshpool. (Desmond Coakham)

No.822 has run round the special train at Llanfair Caereinion. When BR closed the railway in 1956 both the original locomotives, *The Earl* and *The Countess*, were stored at Welshpool before being moved to Oswestry Works. The pair were purchased by the preservation society for £654 with No.1 returning in 1961 and No.2 the following year. (Desmond Coakham)

Llanfair Caereinion station had no watering facilities and the Great Western built a stream-fed water tower beside the River Banwy half a mile from Llanfair. No.822 is seen taking water here in June 1956 on the return journey to Welshpool. The water tower remained in use until 1987. (Desmond Coakham)

In 1962 a Hibberd 'Planet' diesel was purchased from the Admiralty's Lodge Hill & Upnor Railway. As the railway's only big diesel locomotive, it proved invaluable on permanent way trains and as a shunter. Named *Upnor Castle* it is seen in Llanfair Caereinion yard in 1962. Its short wheelbase made it a rough rider and it was sold to the Festiniog Railway in 1968 (see page 69). (Paul Chancellor Collection)

By 13 July 1968 *The Earl* had been repainted in lined Great Western green livery. It is seen here at Llanfair Caereinion with No.3, *Raven*, a 16/20hp Ruston & Hornsby diesel. In the platform is the rake of ex-Zillertalbahn four-wheel coaches that arrived from Austria in April 1968.

The Countess has arrived at Llanfair Caereinion on 13 July 1968 with the combination car. To provide a contrast with *The Earl*, No.2 has been painted in Cambrian Railways' lined black, despite carrying a GWR polished brass safety valve bonnet.

In 1971 the railway purchased a 1927-built Kerr Stuart 0-6-2T from the Antigua Sugar Co. in the West Indies. It arrived in Wales in November and entered service in 1977. Two years later on 12 August 1979 No.12, by now named *Joan*, is at Castle Caereinion with a train for Llanfair.

As well as buying a rake of coaches from Austria in 1968, an ex-Feldbahn 0-8-0T was obtained from Weiz depot in December 1969. With 13,535lb of tractive effort it was the most powerful engine on the line. Named *Sir Drefaldwyn* – the Welsh for Montgomeryshire – it is seen entering Llanfair with a heavy summer train made up of ex-Admiralty and Zillertalbahn stock

Left: Despite the purchase of locomotives from abroad, the two original locomotives are still important members of the motive power fleet. No.1, *The Earl*, is seen approaching the temporary terminus and passing loop at Sylfaen with a train from Llanfair in 1977.

Below: Acquired in 1966 from Bowaters of Sittingbourne, Bagnall-built 0-4-4-0T *Monarch* is seen running round at Llanfair Caereinion in 1976. An indifferent steamer, it only worked between 1973 and 1978 and was sold to the Festiniog Railway in 1992. It has now returned to the W&LLR and has been cosmetically restored for display purposes.

The 1944-built ex-German WD 0-8-0T *Sir Drefaldwyn* is leaving Llanfair with a train of mixed passenger stock. This view of Llanfair station makes an interesting comparison with that on page 12.

In 1975 this handsome Hunslet 2-6-2T was purchased from the Sierra Leone Railway. No.14 entered service at Easter 1979 and is seen the following year running round at Llanfair station. The 2-6-2T has proved to be a powerful and economic addition to the Welshpool's locomotive fleet.

On 18 July 1981 the railway re-opened to Raven Square, Welshpool. The section of line between Sylfaen and Raven Square includes Golfa Bank, with gradients as severe as 1 in 29. On 19 August 2002 2-6-2T No.15, *Orion*, is drifting down the 1 in 33 gradient into Sylfaen with a train for Llanfair.

The sale of *Upnor Castle* in 1968 was the outcome of the railway acquiring *Chattenden*, a Baguley-Drewry 0-6-0DM diesel. Seen here at Llanfair in August 2002, No.7 was quite capable of working passenger trains in an emergency. In the background is the diminutive Barclay 0-4-0T, *Dougal*, which arrived from the Glasgow Corporation gasworks in 1969.

Orion is seen entering Raven Square station on 19 August 2002. The massive 2-6-2T was acquired from Finland in 1983 and only entered service in June 2000. The train, made up of Austrian and Sierra Leone coaches, has safely negotiated the descent of the 1 in 29 Golfa Bank.

The railway acquired this Baguley-Drewry four-wheel ex-military inspection vehicle No. 9150 in 2008 for use by its permanent way department and is seen at Llanfair in September 2009.

No. 823 *Countess* in GWR unlined green livery rests between duties having just taken water at Raven Square in June 2009 from the ex-Pwllheli water tower before heading a passenger train to Llanfair.

Departing for Llanfair Caereinion *Orion* makes an impressive sight as it leaves the ex-Eardisley station buildings at Raven Square. When opened in 1981 Raven Square was just a temporary platform and run round loop. Now the station boasts a full complement of passenger and locomotive facilities.

Two

Vale of Rheidol Railway

Running from Aberystwyth to Devil's Bridge through the valley of the Afon Rheidol, the Vale of Rheidol (VoR) Railway opened in 1902. Davies & Metcalfe of Manchester supplied two 2-6-2Ts, Edward VII and Prince of Wales, and in 1903 a second-hand 2-4-0T, Rheidol, was acquired. The railway's independent existence ceased in 1913 when it was absorbed by Cambrian Railways and in 1922 yet another change occurred when it became part of the Great Western Railway.

The GWR updated the railway's rolling stock, building three new 2-6-2Ts as well as new bogie passenger coaches. The company promoted the Vale of Rheidol as a tourist attraction and the passenger service survived closure during the Second World War. Upon nationalisation the line passed into British Railways' hands and, after 1968, the three 2-6-2Ts were the last steam locomotives owned by BR, being unique in carrying corporate blue livery. For many years rumours abounded that the line was to be closed or sold and eventually, on 30 March 1989, the railway was sold to the owners of the Brecon Mountain Railway for £306,500. The new owners have since spent a great deal of money on redressing the years of neglect that were the precursor to British Rail's disposing of the line.

Swindon-built locomotives No.8 Llywelyn and No.9 Prince of Wales are prepared for duty outside the original corrugated iron engine shed which was located alongside the closed harbour branch. (Desmond Coakham)

2-6-2T No.7 *Owain Glyndŵr* is ready to leave Aberystwyth with a train for Devil's Bridge. The original VoR station was behind the photographer while the mainline station can be seen in the background. Llywelyn carries lined BR green livery while the coaches are all in chocolate and cream. (Desmond Coakham)

No.9 *Prince of Wales* takes water at Aberffrwd, the main intermediate station on the line. The train has climbed 200ft from Aberystwyth and faces a climb of 480ft in four miles before reaching Devil's Bridge. (Desmond Coakham)

Leaving Aberffrwd *Prince of Wales* attacks the 1 in 50 gradient. Weighing 25 tons and with 9,615lb of tractive effort available, No.9 will use almost all the 520 gallons of water in its tanks to reach Devil's Bridge. (Desmond Coakham)

By 1964 the chocolate and cream coach paintwork had given way to what was loosely termed Cambrian Railways bronze. With its train in this livery, No.9 is pictured at Devil's Bridge waiting to return to Aberystwyth.

The Vor 2-6-2Ts were compact and powerful locomotives for a 1ft 11 ½ in gauge railway as No.9 *Prince of Wales*, resplendent in lined green livery, illustrates outside the old GWR shed on Monday, 1 August 1960.

The 1968 season saw VoR trains using the Carmarthen bay of the mainline station at Aberystwyth. The engine shed was also converted to house the narrow gauge locomotives and coaches. *Prince of Wales*, by now painted dull rail blue, raises steam in the early 1970s.

Above: On 25 April 1973 No.7, *Owain Glyndwr*, passes between the engine shed and water tower at Aberystwyth with a loaded train for Devil's Bridge. By this date the VoR was BR's only steam-operated line.

Right: Prince of Wales runs into the cutting at the entrance to Devil's Bridge station past the water tower. To take water the locomotives had to reverse out of the station to this point.

Left: Prince of Wales runs into Devil's Bridge station, 680ft above sea level and almost twelve miles from Aberystwyth. Devil's Bridge, really three bridges on top of each other, crosses the gorge of the Afon Mynach, a local beauty spot.

Below: A busy afternoon scene at Devil's Bridge as No.8, *Llywelyn,* arrives from Aberystwyth while *Prince of Wales* is waiting to depart for the coast.

No.8 *Llywelyn* has run round, taken water and is about to couple up to its returning working to Aberystwyth. The fireman is acting as shunter while the driver keeps a watchful eye on proceedings.

The very basic station at Devil's Bridge is quiet as No.8 *Llywelyn* awaits departure for Aberystwyth. In 1976 the three 2-6-2Ts began to be converted to oil firing because of the risk to the Forestry Commission plantation through which the line runs.

In 1982 No.9 was re-painted in yellow ochre and red by BR, the original Cambrian Railways livery. Under a clear blue sky No.9 *Prince of Wales* prepares to leave Aberystwyth with a train of blue coaches at Spring Bank.

No.9, resplendent in its yellow livery, takes water at Aberffrwd where the rhododendrons are coming into bloom. The picture makes an interesting comparison with that on page 22 taken a quarter of a century earlier.

Rather belatedly BR attempted to improve the 2-6-2Ts blue paintwork by lining them out in white and black. In this revised livery No.7 *Owain Glyndwr* is pictured at Devil's Bridge.

In 1986 No.8 was repainted in Cambrian black livery. On 30 May 1989 the now nameless 2-6-2T has just arrived at Devil's Bridge and is about to run round its train, by now back in GWR livery.

After being sold in 1989, the VoR's new owners set to work to make good the backlog of maintenance that had occurred under BR. On 9 August 2001, maroon liveried and air-braked *Prince of Wales* sets off from Aberystwyth. The train is dwarfed by a Somerfield supermarket built on the site of the earlier terminus (see page 22).

Great Western liveried No.8 is crossing the Rheidol Bridge on 17 August 2002 with a lightly loaded train bound for Devil's Bridge. The immaculate condition of the locomotive and train is a credit to the line's owners.

Three

Talyllyn Railway

Opened in 1866 the 2ft 3in gauge Talyllyn Railway was built to carry slate from the Bryn Eglwys quarries to the Cambrian Railway at Towyn. Owned by the Aberdovey Slate Co. it was also permitted to carry passngers between Abergynolwyn and Towyn Pendre. Two Fletcher Jennings locomotives, Talyllyn and Dolgoch, were sufficient to handle the traffic.

In 1911 the local MP, Haydn Jones, bought the railway and quarries and, despite mixed fortunes, managed to keep the railway running until his death, aged eighty-six, on 2 July 1950. Were it not for a group of enthusiasts led by L.T.C. Rolt, the Talyllyn would have closed and been sold for scrap. Sir Haydn's executors allowed the fledgling preservation society to run trains in 1951, after which his widow donated the railway to the Talyllyn Preservation Society.

In the half century since it became a pioneer preserved railway, the Talyllyn has consolidated its position. Additional steam and diesel locomotives have arrived, as have passenger coaches and goods wagons. New standard coaches have been built and there has been a gradual upgrading of station facilities. In 1976 the line was extended from Abergynolwyn to Nant Gwernol. In 2005 a new and enlarged station and museum building was opened at Tywyn Wharf Station by Their Royal Highnesses the Prince of Wales and the Duchess of Cornwall. 2010 marked the 60th anniversary of the Talyllyn Railway's preservation by volunteers and the only working locomotive, Dolgoch, was returned to traffic, complete with new boiler, for the celebrations.

2001 marked the 50th anniversary of the founding of the Talyllyn Preservation Society. To mark the occasion, the 137-year-old No.1 *Talyllyn* carries a commemorative headboard as it awaits departure from Towyn Wharf to Nant Gwernol on 7 August 2001. The Fletcher Jennings 0-4-2ST is now air-braked.

Above: Ex-Corris Railway No.3 *Sir Haydn* runs round its train at Towyn Wharf station on 14 September 1970. In the foreground is the ex-Irish Turf Board 3ft gauge *Andrew Barclay* 0-4-2T that was to be re-built and named *Tom Rolt*.

Left: At 135 years old, *Dolgoch* is the Talyllyn Railway's other Fletcher Jennings locomotive. Carrying a commemorative headboard, the 0-4-0T is seen at Wharf on 7 August 2001 during the 50th anniversary year.

Tom Rolt entered service in May 1991 and has proved to be a welcome addition to the Talyllyn's motive power. On a clear but snowy 28 December 2000, No.7 is ready to leave Towyn Wharf with a Christmas working to Nant Gwernol.

The Talyllyn's other ex-Corris locomotive is 0-4-0ST No.4 *Edward Thomas* built in 1921 by Kerr Stuart. No.4 is seen at the redeveloped Wharf station on a very wet afternoon in June 2008 preparing to leave with a train for Nant Gwernol.

Dolgoch catches the low winter sun as it runs round at Towyn Wharf on 29 December 1999. The locomotive has been fitted with an air pump and painted in light green.

Towyn Wharf on 18 August 2002 makes an interesting comparison with the picture on page 32. The booking office has just been re-constructed as part of the on-going development of the station while the café and Narrow Gauge Railway Museum are seen in the background. *Talyllyn* awaits the right of way.

34

Edward Thomas was re-boilered in 1964 and in 1976 its frames were lengthened while the valve gear was strengthened. No.4 is waiting to leave Wharf for Nant Gwernol on 10 August 1978 and makes an interesting comparison to its Corris days (page 117).

On 7 August 2001 *Talyllyn* is seen leaving Wharf and about to pass under the Aberdovey to Tywyn main road and enter the cutting leading to Pendre. The leading coach is one of the railway's standard bogie carriages.

Left: Cambrai, a metre gauge 0-6-0T built in 1888, arrived at Towyn on 12 December 1960 and was displayed outside the Narrow Gauge Railway Museum where it is seen on 14 September 1970. It remained here until 1975, being moved to the Irchester Narrow Gauge Railway Museum in 1983.

Seen at Wharf on 14 September 1970 is *Andrew Barclay* No.2268 of 1948, which was built for the Irish Turf Board. Having arrived in Wales during 1969, the driving wheels have been removed for re-gauging. The locomotive is now running as *Tom Rolt* (see page 33).

The *Talyllyn* has a fleet of small diesel locomotives which are used for engineering trains. No.5 *Midlander* is a standard Ruston-Hornsby four-wheel shunter and is seen at Wharf on 31 August 1971. The bridge in the background carries the road to the seafront over the ex-Cambrian Railways main line to Machynlleth.

Returning to Towyn with a Christmas working on 29 December 2001, *Tom Rolt* is barely recognisable as the 0-4-2T that arrived from Ireland in 1969. The *Talyllyn*'s fully lined-out green livery is ideally suited to the locomotive's lines.

Above: Alf was built by the Hunslet Engine Co. for underground use at Huncoat Colliery in Lancashire. It arrived on the Talyllyn in December 1970 and, despite only having a top speed of 9mph, has proved a very useful acquisition. It is pictured in Wharf yard on 16 August 2002.

Left: Between Wharf and Pendre stations the line climbs through a steep-sided cutting. No.6 *Douglas* is seen tackling the 1 in 120 gradient as it approaches School Road Bridge with a five-coach working in the summer of 1978.

Talyllyn has steam to spare and is about to pass under School Road Bridge with a train of bogie coaches. Pendre, which means the end of town, is a little under half a mile from Wharf station.

Drivers of down trains had to be careful of the 1 in 120/150 gradient descent into Wharf station as, until the fitting of air brakes in the late 1990s, the only brakes were those on the locomotive and brake van. *Douglas* is about to enter Wharf station at walking pace on 27 July 1968.

Douglas runs into Pendre station on 31 July 1968. The original passenger buildings are to the right while to the left is the works building.

The works yard at Pendre is seen on 18 August 2002. In the foreground is *Bryneglwys*, a four-wheeled Simplex built for surface work at a coal mine that was bought in 1997. With a top speed of 15mph it can deputise for failed steam locomotives in emergencies.

Above: Rhydyronen, the first intermediate station to be built on the Talyllyn, is two miles from Wharf. *Douglas* is seen arriving with an up train in the 1970s.

Right: Another view of Rhydyronen sees *Dolgoch* arriving with a passenger working. Until 1974 there was a small siding to the north of the running line which served the local mines.

Above: At Brynglas there is a passing loop and siding as well as a block post built to increase the capacity of the single-track line. On a busy summer's day *Talyllyn* passes a down train whose last coach is Corris No.17, which is used as an observation car.

Left: At Dolgoch the railway crosses the Nant Dolgoch ravine on a spectacular viaduct. On 16 August 1974 No.2 *Dolgoch* crosses the viaduct with a train bound for Abergynolwyn.

Right: On 11 August 1979 No.4 *Edward Thomas* crosses the three-arch Dolgoch Viaduct with a train bound for Nant Gwernol. The train has now climbed 152ft in the four miles from Wharf station and will take water at Dolgoch station.

Below: Dolgoch has just taken water at Dolgoch station and is about to depart for Abergynolwyn on 16 August 1974. The station is at the centre of a number of woodlands around the Dolgoch Waterfalls.

8 August 2001 finds No.6 *Douglas* masquerading as the Revd Wilbert Awdry's children's railway book character *Dougal* at Dolgoch. The Revd Awdry was a volunteer of the Talyllyn Railway.

Abergynolwyn on 31 July 1968 has changed little from its pre-preservation days as *Dolgoch* brings a heavy train of mixed stock to a halt. The stone shelter provides the only passenger facilities. Consequently the first vehicle behind the engine is a refreshment bar which will return to Towyn with the day's last train.

No.3 *Sir Haydn* hurries its train towards Abergynolwyn. The temporary sidings in the foreground were used for holding construction skips during the upgrading of the section of line from Abergynolwyn to Nant Gwernol.

By 1978 Abergynolwyn had been transformed into an important passing loop with a café, shop and signal box as well as a 620ft-long platform capable of holding both up and down trains simultaneously. Here *Douglas* is leaving with a train for Nant Gwernol. The first three coaches are four-wheelers supplied in 1866.

Evidence of the upgrading of Abergynolwyn is apparent in this view of *Dolgoch* arriving in the mid-1970s. The running line and loop have been re-laid with hardwood sleepers but the ballasting has yet to be consolidated.

The opposite end of Abergynolwyn station sees *Sir Haydn* arriving with a down train from Nant Gwernol. The open coaches are very popular with the travelling public on sunny days such as this and provide excellent views of the countryside.

The timeless fascination of the steam locomotive. *Talyllyn* is the centre of attraction at the bottom end of Abergynolwyn station in the late 1970s as it waits for the arrival of an up working.

A few minutes after the top picture was taken an up working behind *Sir Haydn* passes *Talyllyn*'s train and will cross over into the platform road using the points behind the photographer.

Left: Dolgoch runs round at Nant Gwernol having climbed 234ft from Towyn Wharf during the 7 ¼ mile trip from the coast. To the right of the station is the steep valley of the Nant Gwernol.

Right: Bound for Nant Gwernol, *Douglas* accelerates its train into the woods for the last mile of the up journey. Opened in 1976, Nant Gwernol is as the heart of a series of scenic footpaths that are very popular with walkers.

Four

Fairbourne Railway

The origins of the Fairbourne Railway date back to 1890 when the builders developing Fairbourne built a 2ft gauge horse tramway. On completion of the housing in 1895 the tramway was extended to Porth Penrhyn to connect with the Barmouth ferry. Two toastrack carriages were the only rolling stock.

In 1915 the line closed and was re-gauged to 15in, re-opening the following year. Motive power consisted of Prince Edward of Wales, a Basset-Lowke Improved Little Giant 4-4-2. In 1923 it was replaced by the Heywood-designed Katie which was quickly superseded by another Basset-Lowke 4-4-2, Prince Louis, in 1925. An 18in gauge 4-2-2 was purchased in 1926 for when Prince Louis was out of traffic. This, however, involved laying dual gauge track. Eventually the 4-2-2 was disposed of in 1936 after the arrival of a Lister diesel, Whippet Quick, in 1935.

The railway closed in 1940 and was sold in 1946. A complete re-build was necessary before passengers could be carried again in 1948. Additional locomotives arrived in the 1950s and 1960s. However, the line was sold once more in 1985 to John Ellerton and converted to 12 ¼ in gauge. Another sale in 1995 to Dr Roger Melton and Professor Tony Atkinson has seen a gradual upturn in the Fairbourne Railway's fortunes.

Sian at Barmouth Ferry in August 1979. Built by Guest Engineering in 1963 Sian was delivered to Fairbourne in 1964 and became one of the mainstays of the Fairbourne's motive power for twenty years.

Fairbourne Station on 1 August 1960 with Bassett-Lowke 4-4-2 *Count Louis* being made ready to depart for Barmouth Ferry. Bo-Bo diesel *Dingo* is stabled in the carriage siding to the right of the picture. (J.A. Peden)

Prince Charles was a scale model of an LMS Black Five and was loaned to the Fairbourne Railway for the 1960 and 1961 seasons. Although a handsome-looking engine in maroon livery, it was a poor steamer and is seen here ready to leave Fairbourne on 26 May 1961. (M.J. Messenger)

Dingo is seen running into Fairbourne Station on 26 May 1961 with a lightly loaded train from Barmouth Ferry. *Dingo* went to Fairbourne in 1952 and was fitted with this stylish body in 1954. However, by 1969 it was out of use and was scrapped in 1974. (M.J. Messenger)

Inside the train shed at Fairbourne with *Dingo* arriving with a train of open carriages. The train shed was large enough to allow much of the Fairbourne's rolling stock to be kept under cover. (Hugh Davies Collection)

During the 1950s and 1960s the Fairbourne was well equipped with diesel locomotives. Here *Dingo* and *Whippet Quick* are at Barmouth. Both have remarkably stylish bodywork for the period. Unfortunately both were out of use by 1969. (Hugh Davies Collection)

Between 1961 and 1984 the railway operated this 4-6-2, built for Dudley Zoo and named *Ernest W. Twining* after its designer. Here the blue pacific is running round at Fairbourne. Behind the tender can be seen the Cambrian Railways line to Barmouth and Machynlleth.

Right: Katie is seen striding out alongside Beach Road. Built in 1954, *Katie* originally worked at Dudley Zoo, not arriving at Fairbourne until 1965. *Katie* and *Sian* are to all intents and purposes identical except for the shape of their domes, *Katie's* being taller than that fitted to *Sian*.

Below: Count Louis is seen among the sand dunes at Barmouth Ferry coupled to its 1953 tender. Named after Count Louis Zborowski, the locomotive ran at Fairbourne from 1925 to 1987.

On what appears to be a chilly summer's day *Katie* threads her way through the sand dunes en route to Barmouth Ferry. This section of line between the golf course and the ferry was very susceptible to becoming inundated with sand in bad weather.

Journey's end – Barmouth Ferry on 11 August 1979. Behind *Sian* are the waters of the Afon Mawddach and Barmouth itself. A regular ferry service crosses the Mawddach Estuary to Barmouth at this point.

Almost a driver's eye view from *Sian*'s cab on 11 August 1979. The clean lines of the 'Twining Twins' suggest the design was inspired by some of William Dean's Great Western locomotives of the late nineteenth century.

On 11 August 1979 the Fairbourne Railway held an open day when all the steam locomotives were in use. Here *Count Louis* pilots *Ernest W. Twining* towards Barmouth Ferry.

Returning to Fairbourne, the double-headed train seen in the previous picture is now running with the locomotives tender-first, with *Ernest W. Twining* leading *Count Louis*.

Operation of the Fairbourne Railway as a 12 ¼ in gauge line commenced on 28 March 1986. On 15 August 1986 2-6-4T *Russell* is on the Fairbourne traverser. *Russell* began life as a replica Leek & Manifold Railway 2-6-4T and was re-built in this configuration in 1984/5.

In this three-quarters rear view, *Russell* bares a more than passing resemblance to the Welsh Highland Hunslet 2-6-2T of the same name seen on page 102.

0-6-4T *Beddgelert* takes water at Fairbourne on 22 August 1998. This locomotive is a half-size replica based on the North Wales Narrow Gauge Railway's own *Beddgelert*.

By the date of this photograph, 22 August 1998, the station and rolling stock at Fairbourne has changed out of all recognition when compared to the picture on page 50.

The driver looking out of the cab of *Yeo* emphasises the change in the Fairbourne Railway from a true narrow gauge line to a miniature railway. *Yeo* is running round at Penrhyn Point (Barmouth Ferry) on 31 May 1991.

This is the view of Penrhyn Point station that greets passengers who have just disembarked from the Barmouth ferry on 31 May 1991, as replica Lynton & Barnstaple Railway 2-6-2T *Yeo* runs round its rake of red carriages.

Departing from Penryhn Point *Yeo* has steam to spare. The 12 ¼ in gauge coaches are really quite narrow and a tight fit for an adult to squeeze into, as this picture testifies.

Beddgelert has passed Pont Penrhyn and is heading towards the dunes and Penrhyn Point with a heavy train on 22 August 1998.

Returning from Penrhyn Point and heading towards Pont Penrhyn, *Russell* is working hard to keep its seven-coach train on the move, 22 August 1998.

Five

Festiniog Railway

Opened on 20 April 1836, the Festiniog Railway (FR) was built to provide the quarries at Blaenau Ffestiniog with an efficient way of transporting slate to the coast. The original horse and gravity trains became unable to meet the demand of the quarry owners and four small steam locomotives, The Princess, Mountaineer, The Prince and Palmerston were bought in 1863/4. Passengers were officially not carried until 1865 but as traffic increased in 1867 two larger 0-4-0STTs, Welsh Pony and Little Giant, were obtained. The first double Fairlie, Little Wonder, was delivered in 1869 and was followed by the improved engines James Spooner, Taliesin, Merddin Emrys and Livingston Thompson.

However after the expansion years of the nineteenth century, the first half of the twentieth century saw the Festiniog's fortunes go into decline, so much so that on Friday 15 September 1939 all passenger trains were withdrawn. Slate traffic continued until 1 August 1946, when the railway closed. Fortunately, like the Talyllyn, a group of enthusiasts gained control of the railway in 1954 and it was then re-opened in stages from 1955. Tan-y-Bwlch was reached in 1958, Dduallt in 1968 and Blaenau Ffestiniog in 1982. Such has been the progress over the last fifty years that the Festiniog can once more rightly claim to be the premier narrow gauge railway. In 2010 the connection with the Welsh Highland Railway was reinstated and once more narrow gauge trains can be seen crossing the Britannia Bridge after a gap of more than 70 years.

Merddin Emrys brings an afternoon train from Tan-y-Bwlch across the Cob towards Portmadoc on 8 August 1964. *Merddin Emrys* was built at Boston Lodge in 1879 and had returned to steam in 1961 after fifteen years out of use.

Turtle roof bogie van No.3 and a box van are seen at Harbour Station on 8 June 1954. When the Festiniog closed down on 1 August 1946 the rolling stock was simply left where it stood and this was the result. Happily, a replica curly roof van has been built at Boston Lodge allowing the FR once more to use one of these iconic vehicles in its vintage trains. (Desmond Coakham)

Double Fairlie *Taliesin* is in Boston Lodge Works yard along with Harrogate Gaswork's Peckett *Volunteer* in March 1956. The Peckett was never used on the FR while *Taliesin* worked from 1956 until 1971 and is now at the National Railway Museum in York restored to its 1885 condition as *Livingston Thompson*. (R.J. Leonard KRM)

Prince was the first steam locomotive to be restored to traffic by the new Festiniog Co. in August 1955. Here it is seen with a typical three-coach working of the period. (Hugh Davies Collection)

The big event of 1961 was the return to steam of *Merddin Emrys*. Seen shunting stock at Harbour Station in August 1961, the double Fairlie is running in red primer without its cab or spectacle plates. (R.J. Leonard KRM)

Blanche is running round at Portmadoc in 1974. At this time the station buildings at Harbour were being extended to provide a buffet and enlarged shop.

On 12 September 1970 *Mountaineer* is approaching Rhiw Plas Bridge with a train bound for Dduallt. The Cob can be seen in the background.

An apparently deserted Tan-y-Bwlch is the setting for this view of *Linda* on the 12.45 p.m. working from Blaenau Ffestiniog on 15 August 1986.

Between 1969 and 1978 Dduallt was the upper terminus of the Festiniog. In this view a much rebuilt *Merddin Emrys* is seen departing with a down working to Portmadoc.

Left: The line between Moelwyn Tunnel and Tan-y-Grisiau hugs the eastern shore of Llyn Ystradau. *Mountaineer* is rounding one of the curves between the power station summit and Tan-y-Grisiau.

Below: In August 1981 *Prince* and *Blanche* head a heavy down train out of Tan-y-Grisiau. By this time *Prince* was only used on light trains or as a pilot on the heaviest workings.

Mountaineer is about to depart for Portmadoc from Tan-y-Grisiau on 23 August 1978. Tan-y-Grisiau served as the top terminus from 1978 to 1982 and is now only an intermediate station.

The Festiniog Railway runs a number of special events each year aimed at the enthusiast market. During October 1996 Vintage Gala *Linda* pilots *Prince* away from Portmadoc.

Left: Although famed for its steam locomotives, the Festiniog has a number of interesting diesels. Here *Moelwyn*, an ex-WD Baldwin tractor now running as a 2-4-0, is in Boston Lodge yard on 11 July 1968.

Below: Another ex-WD diesel is the four-wheel Simplex, named *Mary Ann*, which is seen here at Tan-y-Bwlch with a short permanent way train.

Right: 1967-built Funkey *Vale of Ffestiniog* was rebuilt by the Festiniog Railway in 1998 and is seen on 22 October 2001 at Minffordd with a train for Blaenau Ffestiniog.

Below: For many years *Upnor Castle* was the only diesel capable of working passenger trains. Here the Hibberd is seen at Portmadoc with a short four-coach working. *Upnor Castle* is barely recognisable as the locomotive illustrated on page 13. It has now been transferred to the WHR(C) where it is used on construction trains between Rhyd Ddu and Pont Croesor.

On 6 April 1994 another Hibberd diesel rebuilt in a totally different style, *Conway/Conwy Castle*, runs into Portmadoc with a five-coach working.

Palmerston was restored in 1994 and is seen outside the original Boston Lodge engine shed during the 1999 Vintage Gala.

The 1999-built single Fairlie *Taliesin* is seen taking water at Blaenau Ffestiniog in March 2000. Owing to the escalating prices of oil it, along with double Fairlies *Earl of Merioneth* and *Merddin Emrys*, has been successfully converted to burn coal.

Single Fairlie *Taliesin* departs from Minffordd with a vintage train comprising original Festiniog passenger stock.

The Santa Specials of December 2010 were run in a winter wonderland of snow as North Wales was badly affected by the blizzards of late November and early December. On 9 December *Iarll Meirionydd* passes Boston Lodge with an up working. (Chris Parry/FRCo.)

During the winter of 2010-11 the Festiniog Railway's main line was cut on the Penrhyn side of the Minffordd to allow a bridge to be installed over the Porthmadog by-pass. Here we see the first train on reconnected line departing from Minffordd 2 March 2011 behind *Merddin Emrys*. (Andrew Thomas/FRCo.)

Six

Snowdon Mountain Railway

The Snowdon Mountain Railway has many claims to fame. It is the only rack-and-pinion railway in Britain, it has a gauge of 2ft 7 ½ in, and it was opened and closed on the same day, Easter Monday 1896, after Ladas derailed and plunged down the mountainside. Re-opened on 19 April 1897, the line was worked by four Swiss-built locomotives. Three more locomotives to a modified design were supplied in 1923. All the coaches were built in England and had one bogie fitted with a brake pinion.

Trains have run every year, weather permitting, except between 1943 and 1945. Despite arrears of maintenance and financial problems having to be surmounted, the railway is as popular as ever. In 1986 two Hunslet diesel locomotives were delivered, with two more following in 1991 and 1992, allowing more trains to run at reduced costs. In 1995 a three-car diesel electric railcar was built by HPE Tredegar which, after initial teething troubles, has provided even greater operating flexibility. In its first century the Snowdon Mountain Railway has carried an estimated 5 ½ million people the 4 ½ miles from Llanberis to the summit on a ruling gradient of 1 in 5 ½. Now well into its second century, the railway continues to fulfil its original function of carrying the general public to the summit of Wales' highest mountain.

A shaft of sunlight picks out No.6 *Padarn* as it leaves Llanberis with a coach load of passengers on the first leg of the 4 ½ mile journey to the summit of Snowdon in August 1966. All the locomotives push their single coach, there being no physical connection between the two. *Padarn* was built in 1922 and carries the then standard light green livery of the Snowdon Mountain Railway.

No.2 *Enid* was built in 1895 and is in the locomotive yard at Llanberis. The Snowdon rack locomotives are six-wheeled tank engines with horizontal cylinders which drive the track pinions, not the wheels themselves, which revolve freely on their axles. (J.A. Peden)

No.7, built in 1923 and named *Aylwin*, now carries the name *Ralph* and illustrates the differences in design between the 1895 and 1922/3 locomotives. These have a modified type of Joy valve gear while the early locomotives have Hackworth gear. (J.A. Peden)

Enid and the other Snowdon locomotives all have well tanks on either side of the footplate. The side tanks have two compartments with separate fillers. The front section is for cooling purposes when the compression braking is in operation while descending the mountain. (J.A. Peden)

No.8 *Eryri* illustrates the massive frames of the Snowdon locomotives, which are designed to cope with the massive forces exerted by the cylinders when working flat out on the mountain. This view also clearly shows the radial valve gear fitted to the second batch of engines. (J.A. Peden)

No.4 *Snowdon* is at Llanberis. Schweierische Locomotiv- und Maschinenfabrik at Winterthur, Switzerland, built *Snowdon* in 1896 and this view clearly shows the angle at which the boiler is pitched to allow the water level to remain horizontal while on the mountain.

One of the first batch of locomotives has steam to spare as it pushes its coach across the Upper Viaduct at Llanberis in 1966. Although nominally a 0-4-2T, the wheels just carry the weight of the locomotive as the power is transmitted to the rack and pinion.

With Llyn Padarn in the background Hunslet diesel No.12 *George* propels its train over Upper Viaduct above Llanberis. Although the steam locomotive fleet now carries different liveries the coaches still maintain the Snowdon Mountain Railway's traditional red and cream livery.

Enid is blowing off vigorously as she pushes her single coach towards Hebron. Although capable of handling two coaches, the loading is kept to one coach.

No.4 *Snowdon* has reached Clogwyn Station at Easter 1975 where the day's services were terminated because of snow and ice blocking the line higher up the mountain. The cloud base is clearly visible behind the coach.

The daily works train is at Clogwyn station in charge of No.6 *Padarn*. This working always forms the first train of the day as it conveys water and stores to the summit station and restaurant. The water tank is next to the locomotive.

Viewed from Clogwyn, the Abt system rack and pinion track is seen climbing away towards the clouds and the summit. The line is never flat, ranging from 1 in 50 in Llanberis station to 1 in 5 ½ in places, and the track has steel posts sunk into the trackbed to stop the track creeping down the mountain.

The original coaches were open-sided vehicles but were rebuilt between 1951 and 1958 with fully enclosed sides. Here open coach No.5 is propelled towards the summit by No.5 *Moel Siabod*. (Hugh Davies Collection)

The 1 in 5 gradient is all too apparent as *Moel Siabod* pushes its single coach into the summit station, which is 3,493ft above sea level. In 2009 a new summit hotel will open allowing trains, which during construction work have terminated at Clogwyn, to once more use the summit station. (Hugh Davies Collection)

The Snowdon Mountain Railway owns the freehold of the track and platforms at the summit but leases the Summit Hotel from Gwynedd County Council. *Moel Siabod* is preparing to descend to Llanberis. (Hugh Davies Collection)

Right: Seen returning to Llanberis station, the HPF multiple unit is fitted with large picture windows that give passengers stunning views of Snowdonia when the weather is clear. After some teething troubles the unit is now proving its worth in giving the railway increased flexibility to respond to passenger numbers. Each coach has its own diesel engine and electric motor.

Below: No.11 *Peris* is one of four Hunslet 0-4-0 diesel hydraulic locomotives purchased in the 1990s. As with the steam locomotives, the passenger coach is pushed up the mountainside. A governor automatically applies the brakes on the coaches if the speed exceeds 7 ½ mph or the locomotive runs away.

All of the steam locomotives now carry different liveries. No.4 *Snowdon* has been painted in dark green with vermilion and yellow lining and has just arrived at Llanberis with the works train from the summit.

The engine shed and works for the Snowdon Mountain Railway are next to the station at Llanberis. On 7 August 1996 No.4 *Snowdon*, with a headboard commemorating the railway's centenary, is stabled by the coal stage.

Seven

Great Orme Tramway

Unique among the Welsh narrow gauge, the funicular Great Orme Tramway is worked as two separate lines with passengers having to change trams at Halfway Station. Two trams run on each section; Nos 3 and 4 on the lower tramway and Nos 6 and 7 on the upper. As the winding drum lowers one tram the other is raised.

Built to a gauge of 3ft 6 ½ in, the lower section from Victoria Station to Halfway opened on 31 July 1902. The upper tramway to the summit opened a year later on 8 July 1903. On 23 August 1932 the tramway closed after a serious accident caused the Great Orme Tramway Co. to go into voluntary liquidation. Re-opened on 17 May 1934 by the Great Orme Tramways Co. Ltd, further closure came during the Second World War.

Ownership passed to Llandudno Urban District Corporation on 1 January 1949, and in October 1957 the steam-winding engine was replaced by electric motors. Further changes came in April 1974 and 1996 when, respectively, Aberconwy Borough Council and Conwy County Council assumed control. Such was the backlog of maintenance in 1997-1998 that closure was only averted by an urgent injection of cash. In the last six years almost £5 million has been spent on upgrading the tramway.

Car No.4 built in 1902 by Hurst Nelson of Motherwell, waits to leave the Victoria terminus in June 2008. The trolley poles do not collect power as the tramway is cable operated but connect with the overhead wire allowing signalling and telegraph communications with the car.

Each car weighs 6 ½ tons and has forty-eight seats. No.4 is near the bottom of the steep and narrow Old Road where the 1932 accident occurred. On the 872yd lower tramway the average gradient is 1 in 6 but increases to 1 in 4 in places. Both sections of track have passing loops.

A Mark 1 Ford Consul waits for Car No.5 at the bottom of Old Road. The changes in gradient are seen to good advantage in this view. (M.J. Messenger)

In places the clearances on the lower section of the tramway are very tight, as is shown in this view of car No.4 climbing out of Llandudno along Old Road. Thankfully cars and motorbikes are forbidden here when the tramway is operating, except for access. (Hugh Davies Collection)

Another view of the stone-walled Old Road, this time with car No.5 in operation. The conduit trackwork here is seen to good effect. (Hugh Davies Collection)

Car No.4 climbs through the passing loop at Black Gate en route to Halfway. In the background are the waters of Llandudno Bay. (Hugh Davies Collection)

Car No.5 is on the lower side of Halfway Station waiting to return to Victoria Station. Lifeguards are only fitted to the off-side of the cars.

The upper section of the tramway only rises 148ft and the rails are spiked onto ordinary ballasted sleepers. Car No.6 is seen against the open landscape that characterises this section of the tramway. (Hugh Davies Collection)

There are occasions when the upper section is shrouded in low cloud. In just such conditions car No.6 takes its load of passengers to the Summit Station.

Halfway Station on 19 May 1962 finds car No.7 waiting for passengers. The track and cable arrangements are more railway-like than that on the lower section, which has the cable in a conduit. (M.J. Messenger)

Near the 637ft high Summit Station, Hurst Nelson Car No.6 of 1903 traverses the less steep 1 in 8 gradients of the 827yd top section. So exposed is this section that gales have been known to turn cars over.

Eight

Llanberis/Padarn Lake Railway

The 1ft 11 ½ in gauge Llanberis Lake Railway runs for two miles on the trackbed of the Padarn Railway. Opened in July 1971, it plays a significant role in the tourist economy of Llanberis. The line's origins go back to the mid-1960s when plans to build a railway along the shores of Llyn Padarn were mooted. After deliberation, a scheme evolved to develop a railway from Gilfach Ddu to Penllyn.

When the Dinorwic quarries closed, three redundant Hunslet 0-4-0STs and a Ruston diesel were bought in December 1969. The diesel was overhauled first so that it could be used on construction trains, and it was soon followed by Dolbadarn. The Gilfach Ddu to Cei Llydan section formally opened on 28 May 1971 but public services were delayed until 19 July due to problems with the new coaches. Nevertheless Dolbadarn and three coaches carried more than 30,000 passengers during 1971.

The extension to Penllyn opened in 1972 with Cei Llydan becoming a passing loop. New coaches entered traffic in 1972 with Elidir. Between 1973-1975 Maid Marian was used and Wild Aster assumed the identity of Thomas Bach when restored in 1988. Today the line carries some 60,000 passengers annually and an extension from Gilfach Ddu to opposite the Snowdon Mountain Railway in Llanberis is due to open in 2003.

Less than two months after opening *Dolbadarn* is at the Gilfach Ddu terminus at Llanberis on 9 September 1971.

Dolbadarn rolls into Gilfach Ddu on 9 September 1971 with a lightly loaded train from Cei Llydan. The newly laid track is still only lightly ballasted and a construction train is in the siding to the right.

On a wet 29 May 1972 *Dolbadarn* prepares to depart for Penllyn with a train made up of four enclosed carriages and one open.

Right: Dolbadarn is parked outside the National Slate Museum of Wales at Gilfach Ddu on 28 May 1990.

Below: Dolbadarn leaves Gilfach Ddu for Penllyn in the rain on 29 May. The coaches, which were all constructed in the railway's workshops, only have doors on one side.

Dolbadarn has arrived at Cei Llydan and is waiting to pass a train bound for Penllyn on 28 May 1990. The coaches have been rebuilt with fully glazed windows and doors to a common profile.

Thomas Bach – originally *Wild Aster* – arrives at Cei Llydan with Llyn Padarn to the right on 28 May 1990. The first two coaches are semi-opens only used when the weather is fine.

Spring Bank Holiday 2002 finds all the railway's locomotives on view outside the Slate Museum. From left to right are *Thomas Bach*, *Elidir*, *Dolbadarn* – now painted in yellow ochre livery – and *Una*. (Carrie Thomas)

Dolbadarn and *Elidir* depart from Gilfach Ddu during the Spring Bank Holiday 2002. The only time double-headed trains are run is on gala days, as the small Hunslet 0-4-0ST are more than capable of handling the timetabled workings. (Carrie Thomas)

Above: Una pilots *Dolbadarn* away from Gilfach Ddu. *Una* is owned by the National Slate Museum of Wales and is occasionally steamed and used on the Padarn Lake Railway to keep it in good order. (Carrie Thomas)

Left: A final look at *Dolbadarn* at Gilfach Ddu on 28 May 1990. The Hunslet 0-4-0STs are economical and possess more than enough power to cope with the demands of a railway running along the banks of Llyn Padarn.

Nine

Bala Lake Railway

The Bala Lake Railway occupies part of the trackbed of the Great Western Railway's secondary mainline between Ruabon and Barmouth Junction, which closed on 18 January 1965. The scheme to build 4 ½ miles of 1ft 11 ½ in gauge railway from Llanuwchllyn to Bala Lake Halt along the shores of the lake was announced in 1971. Such was the progress that the first diesel-hauled train ran from Llanuwchllyn to Pentrepiod on 14 August 1972. However, it was to be 1976 before services operated to Bala Lake Halt.

The first motive power was a small Ruston diesel, while from 1973 to 1975 Meirionnydd, a Severn Lamb diesel hydraulic, worked virtually all the trains. In 1975 Maid Marian became the first steam locomotive to work on the railway. Holy War entered traffic in 1979, the same year the canopy from Aberdovey station was erected at Llanuwchllyn. 52,000 passengers travelled in 1978 but this fell to 29,000 in 1987. A renaissance has seen around 40,000 people carried annually. In 1989 plans to extend to the outskirts of Bala alongside the A494 were published, but to date they remain unfulfilled despite the higher profile a Bala terminus would give the railway.

Holy War is being prepared for the first train of the day on 20 August 2002 at Llanuwchllyn. The 0-4-0ST has come off shed and run through the station to take on water and coal. The company, Rheilffordd Lyn Tegid, was the first to be registered in Welsh to build a 2ft gauge railway.

Easter 1974 finds Severn Lamb diesel hydraulic *Meirionnydd* at Llangower with an early season train comprised of an open-sided tourist coach and a bogie brake. *Meirionnydd* was the mainstay of the railway for two years until *Maid Marian* entered traffic.

Holy War drifts into Llangower on 13 August 1979 with a train for Llanuwchllyn comprised of two open and two closed coaches. 1979 was *Holy War*'s first season in traffic on the Bala Lake Railway.

A decade later finds *Maid Marian* approaching Llangower on 28 May 1989. The small Hunslet 0-4-0STs are ideal motive power for the railway, being powerful yet economic, despite having to work much harder than in their Dinorwic quarry days.

Although the railway runs along the shore of Lake Bala – Llyn Tegid – there is a half-mile stretch of line at a gradient of 1 in 70 in the Llanuwchllyn direction. *Holy War* is seen descending Ddolfawr Bank with a train, with the normal loading of four bogie coaches, bound for Bala Lake Halt on 13 August 1979.

20 August 2002 finds *Holy War* at Llanuwchllyn station with the 11.00 a.m. departure for Bala Lake Halt. The load of five coaches will tax the locomotive on the climb up Ddolfawr Bank on the return trip. The first coach includes accommodation for disabled passengers.

Holy War eases through Llangower station on 20 Augusts 2002. Lake Bala is the largest natural lake in Wales and some of the best views are obtained from the train. At Llangower there is a picnic site and lakeside walks. There is a passing loop here but it is now only used on special occasions, as the normal timetable only requires one engine to be in steam.

Ten

Welsh Highland
Heritage Railway

Formed in 1961, the Welsh Highland Railway (WHR) Society set about purchasing the trackbed of the Welsh Highland Railway from the official liquidator. Agreement was reached and a price of £850 negotiated when, before contracts could be exchanged, the liquidator died in September 1964. As a result, work had to start from scratch with the Official Receiver.

In 1973 the 1964 Co., as it had become known, purchased Beddgelert Siding from British Railways. Gerlert's Farm was bought in 1975 and became the company's engineering base. A mile of track was laid from Portmadoc to Pen-y-Mount and in 1987 Russell returned to steam. The Railway had acquired a diverse collection of locomotives, ranging from small diesel mechanical 0-4-0s to Bagnall and Peckett 0-4-2Ts, an ex-South African Railways NG15 2-8-2 and three Polish Lyd 2 0-6-0 diesels. Rolling stock includes some original WHR vehicles that have been restored from derelict condition as well as others sourced from elsewhere.

The company's plans to re-open the WHR were scuppered when it emerged that the Ffestiniog Railway had made a bid to buy the trackbed. In 1995 the Ffestiniog Railway was granted a Light Railway Order to re-build the railway. After the initial anger this caused, by 1998 the two companies had agreed to work together to re-open the WHR. Further disagreements have prevented WHHR rails joining those of the WHR(C) but in 2011 the two companies were more positive about this coming about.

Porthmadog station on 15 August 2002 finds *Russell* at the head of a train for Pen-y-Mount. *Russell* is the only surviving locomotive from the original Welsh Highland Railway.

The best part of seventy-five years separates this picture from that on the previous page. Portmadoc New station is a hive of activity as two trains pass, with *Taliesin* on the left.

We move on into the 1930s at Portmadoc New and find *Merddin Emrys* about to pick up a train bound for the Festiniog Railway, which will pass through the streets of Portmadoc. (R.W. Kidner)

6 August 1996 sees *Russell* running into a deserted Porthmadog with a train from Pen-y-Mount. The ex-Cambrian Railways main line runs parallel with the Welsh Highland Railway at this point.

Six years later and *Russell* brings a well-patronised train into Porthmadog. The second coach behind *Russell* is the Gladstone Car in which W.E. Gladstone is known to have travelled.

When the Festiniog Railway was physically linked to the Welsh Highland in 1923, *Russell* was cut down in an abortive attempt to allow it to pass through Moelwyn Tunnel, and is seen here at Beddgelert.

Russell was restored to traffic at Easter 1987. New tanks were fitted and the original profile of the cab, dome and chimney were restored.

The Welsh Highland (Porthmadog) Railway has a number of diesel locomotives. Inside the shed at Gelert's Farm are *Cnicht*, *Glaslyn* and one of the Railway's ex-Polish Lyd 2 0-6-0DHs.

In June 2008 Bagnall 0-4-2T *Gelert* stands at Porthmadog station with a train for Glert's Farm and Pont Croesor, the short-lived terminus of the line in 2009.

The railway owns a number of medium-sized steam locomotives. *Karen* was built by Pecketts in 1942 and spent all her working life on the Selukwe Park Light Railway in Rhodesia (now Zimbabwe).

The May Bank Holiday in 2010 saw Baldwin 4-6-0T No.778 visit the line from the Leighton Buzzard Light Railway. In the 1920s and 1930s classmate No.590 was in use on the old WHR having been purchased from the War Department by Colonel Stephens.

At Pen-y-Mount the station building is a replica of one of the original Welsh Highland Railway structures, a wooden frame clad in corrugated iron sheet.

Pen-y-Mount station is no longer the end of the WHR(P)'s line as at the beginning of the 2007 season trains once more ran onto the trackbed of the old WHR on the Traeth Mawr. It is here that in 2009 the junction with the Portmadoc to Beddgelert line will be made. At the same time *Russell*, seen here, will have returned to steam after a heavy overhaul.

Left: In what could almost be Aberglaslyn Pass, but is in fact at Gelert's Farm, *Russell* merges into the scenery as it waits to leave for Pen-y-Mount on 15 August 2002.

Below: The way forward. The pyramid peak of *Cnicht* stands sentinel over the original route of the Welsh Highland Railway into Aberglaslyn Pass. In 2009 the rebuilt WHR is scheduled to reopen, allowing passengers to travel once more from Portmadoc to Beddgelert and beyond to Caernarfon.

Eleven

Welsh Highland (Caernarfon) Railway

The Ffestiniog Railway became involved with the Welsh Highland Railway's revival in 1987 when it sought to buy the trackbed. The aim was not only to restore the WHR but also to construct a new section of line on the ex-LNWR route from Dinas to Caernarfon. The granting of a Light Railway Order in 1995 along with a 999-year lease from Gwynedd County Council was to see trains running once more between Dinas and Caernarfon in October 1997.

The Ffestiniog Railway's plans were for a twenty-five-mile railway operated by powerful ex-South African Railways NGG16 2-6-2+2-6-2 Garratts hauling trains of up to twelve coaches. A National Lottery grant of £4.5 million towards the Caernarvon to Rhyd Ddu section kick-started the project. Two Garratts, Nos 138 and 143, and an ex-Port Elizabeth Cement Works Funkey Bo-Bo diesel were overhauled, while Winston Engineering built six coaches. Two more coaches from Alan Keef Engineering were added to the fleet in 2002. However, lighter trains have seen the Ffestiniog's Mountaineer, Blanche and Prince used.

The Dinas to Waunfawr section opened in 2003 and that to Rhyd Ddu in 2003. April 2009 saw the line opened as far as Beddgelert and to Pont Croesor in May 2010. The first through trains to Porthmadog ran in October 2010 with trains crossing the Cambrian main line at Cae Pawb, the only narrow gauge/standard gauge flat crossing in the country before winding their way through the streets of Porthmadog and over the Britannia Bridge to join the Ffestiniog Railway at Harbour Station.

The backdrop to Caernarfon station on the Welsh Highland (Caernarfon) Railway is Caernarfon Castle. In this impressive setting the Festiniog Railway's *Prince* runs round the vintage train on 15 August 2002.

To work the line from Caernarfon to Porthmadog the Festiniog acquired a brace of ex-South African Railways NGG16 2-6-2+2-6-2 Garratts. Here No.138 runs into the terminus with a train from Dinas.

During the peak summer timetable there is a need for two trains, one formed of modern stock and the other a vintage working. Here *Prince* waits at Caernarfon with the vintage train on 15 August 2002.

NGG16 Garratt No.138 runs into Caernarfon on a chilly 20 August 1998. The trackbed here was originally part of the LNWR route to Afon Wen.

Prince drifts down the gradient into Caernarfon with the three-coach vintage train. The use of *Prince* is apt, as the small Festiniog Railway 0-4-0STTs were used over the original WHR in the 1920s and 1930s.

The one that got away – *Moel Tryfan* is seen at Dinas in the summer of 1934. The WHR 0-6-4T survived until October 1954 when it was cut up to raise money to help restore the Festiniog Railway. (R.W. Kidner)

NGG16 No.138 runs round at Dinas. At this point the Garratt is still on the formation of the standard gauge line. However, once under the bridge behind the coaches the route of the old WHR is joined.

Garratt No.138 is outside the engine shed at Dinas. The locomotive has been named *Millennium* to acknowledge the funding provided by the National Lottery Millennium Fund. A third NGG16 class Garratt, No.87, is being overhauled at Boston Lodge ready for the extension of through services to Harbour Station, Portmadoc.

In June 2008 B-B diesel hydraulic Funkey *Caernarfon Castle* runs into Waunfawr at the head of a train for Rhyd Ddu. The open wagon at the head of the train is for bicycles as the railway encourages hikers and cyclists to use its service to access the more remote parts of Snowdonia.

The NGG16 Garratts should be capable of hauling ten coach trains at speeds of up to 25mph. Here No.138 is being gently run in at Glan-y-Pwll on the Festiniog Railway on 3 May 1997 before moving to the WHR.

Winston Engineering constructed the first batch of coaches for the new WHR. Here No.2041 is at Dinas in August 1998. Boston Lodge has since constructed a batch of similar coaches and another vehicle, No.2060, has been acquired from Romania for evaluation.

As well as buying the Garratts, two former South African Railway NG15 2-8-2s were also brought to Wales for restoration. No.133 is pictured at Dinas in 1998 before work started on its overhaul.

0-4-0+0-4-0T Garratt K1, the first Beyer Garratt to be built, runs into Rhyd Ddu at the head of a well-loaded train in June 2009. In temporary plain black livery K1 has now been painted in gloss black and is fully lined out.

In 2009 NGG16 2-6-2+2-6-2T Garratt No.87 was returned to traffic in grey livery and here we see this magnificent locomotive waiting to leave Rhyd Ddu with a train for Caernarfon. No.87 has since been repainted into a maroon livery similar to that used by the Midland Railway and LMS.

Lyd, a 'new build' Lynton & Barnstaple Railway Manning Wardle 2-6-2T, arrives at Beddgelert with the Festiniog Railway's 'Vintage Set' of coaches during Superpower Weekend 2010. (Andrew Thomas/FRCo.)

Right: The Aberglaslyn Pass is one of the most glorious scenic delights of Snowdonia and here we see NGG16 Beyer Garratt No.143 steaming through the tunnels in the Aberglaslyn Pass alongside the Afon Glaslyn. (Roger Dimmick/ FRCo.)

NGG16 Garratt No.87, still in its grey livery, crosses the Cambrian main line at Cae Pawb in early 2010. the signalling for the flat crossing is controlled from the signalling centre at Machynlleth. (Roger Dimmick/FRCo.)

The river crossing at Pont Croesor is seen as MGG Garratt No.87 brings an afternoon train across the bridge over the Afon Glaslyn on the final stage of the journey to Pont Croesor. (Chris Parry/FRCo.)

On 29 September 2010 England 0-4-0ST+T Palmerston brings the Trustees' Train through the streets of Porthmadog and across the Britannia Bridge toward Harbour Station. (Chris Parry/FRCo.)

Twelve

The Corris Railway

The Corris Railway opened in 1858 as the horse-drawn Corris, Machynlleth & River Dovey Tramroad to carry slate from Corris and Aberllefenni to Machynlleth and the River Dovey at Derwenlas. In 1878 three 0-4-0ST steam locomotives were purchased from the Falcon Engine Co. at Loughborough and passengers were officially carried from 1883.

Owned by Imperial Tramways Co. of Bristol, which was part of the Bristol Tramways & Carriage Co., a merger created Bristol Tramways in which the Great Western Railway had an interest. In 1930 the GWR took over the Corris Railway and almost immediately ceased running passenger trains, allowing another of its interests, Crossville buses, to assume a local monopoly.

In 1921 a Kerr Stuart 0-4-2T No.4 arrived and this allowed the withdrawal of Nos 1 and 2. Nos 3 and 4 were able to cope with traffic, and goods trains continued to run until August 1948 when the River Dovey viaduct was damaged, prompting British Railways to close the railway. In 1951 the Talyllyn Railway bought Nos 3 and 4. The remnants of the Corris Railway were disposed of or allowed to return to nature. However, in 1970 a museum was opened in the extant station buildings at Corris. From this small beginning plans were made to reopen part of the railway and these came to fruition on 3 June 2002 when passengers were again carried between Corris and Maespoeth. Work is under way on the southern extension of the line towards Tan-y-Coed.

When W.A. Camwell photographed No.4 at Corris in 1941 there were only three trains a week along the Dulas Valley. Corris station was provided with an overall roof, which appears to be in good repair. This part of the station is now occupied by a doctor's surgery.

The Corris station at Machynlleth was alongside that of the Cambrian Railway and interchange facilities were provided. In this Frith postcard one of the Falcon Works 0-4-0STs, re-built as a 0-4-2ST, awaits departure for Corris. The train is made up of five centre entrance bogie coaches of which two are extant, one at Corris and No.17 on the Talyllyn.

An unidentified 0-4-2ST, probably No.3, is outside the engine shed at Maespoeth. The Corris locomotives were painted maroon and were only fitted with right-hand cab doors as they all faced uphill. When converted to 0-4-2STs, the opportunity was taken to enlarge the cabs.

W.A. Camwell photographed what is thought to be one of the last trains run by British Railways in August 1948. No.4 awaits departure from Aberllefenni with a load of slates for Machynlleth. This locomotive is now on the Talyllyn Railway and running as No.4 *Sir Haydn*.

Although not strictly a Corris Railway scene, *Sir Haydn* is seen at Towyn Wharf station on the Talyllyn in August 2002 carrying a red livery. The main differences since its Corris days are the modified cab and air compressor, the Corris engines being fitted with vacuum brakes.

In October 1996 Corris Railway Kerr Stuart 0-4-2ST No.4, now the Talyllyn Railway's *Edward Thomas*, returned to Corris to celebrate its 75th anniversary. Unable to operate passenger trains as the Corris Railway as it still awaited the necessary documentation, the locomotive was restricted to hauling a demonstration goods train, seen here between Maespoeth and Corris.

3 June 2002 saw the first passenger train worked by the present company. On Sunday 18 August 2002 Ruston-Hornsby four-wheel diesel No.6 arrives at Corris with the stock for the 11.00 a.m. departure to Maespoeth. A replica Kerr Stuart 0-4-2T was delivered to the railway in May 2005 and the construction of a new Falcon 0-4-2T is now under way.

Above: Ruston-Hornsby four-wheel diesel No.6 is at Corris with the 11.00 a.m. departure for Maespoeth on 18 August. The train comprises all the available passenger stock, the Tiger coach, a four-wheel version of the original bogie coaches, and a brake van. The portacabin at the end of the platform is the local doctor's surgery.

Right: 0-4-2ST No.4 is seen at Maespoeth during its October 1996 visit. Since being acquired by the Talyllyn Railway, No.4 has received a running plate, improved valve gear, a new boiler, an air compressor as well as other improvements. On 23 August 2005 0-4-2T No.7, built to the same design as No.4 when new, entered traffic giving the Corris Railway its first new steam engine for over eighty years.

Maespoeth engine shed in August 2002 looking towards Corris. At present trains terminate at the platform by the shed. Although alongside the A487, there is no public access here and all trains have to be boarded at Corris. A new carriage shed has been built here since this photograph was taken in order to store the railway's increasing number of coaches.

Looking down the Dulas Valley towards Machynlleth from Maespoeth. Work has already started on extending the Corris Railway south to Tan-y-Coed close to the Centre for Alternative Technology, which is a major tourist attraction in this part of Wales.

Thirteen

Gone But Not Forgotten

Although North Wales is endowed with a fascinating variety of narrow gauge railways, there are a number of railways that survived into the 1960s but did not pass into the hands of preservation groups. Among the most notable of these were the Nantlle Railway, Penrhyn Railway, Padarn Railway and the system that served the Dinorwic quarries.

The Nantlle Railway was unique in that it remained horse-worked until closure in 1963, a small matter of 135 years. Luckily, although the Penrhyn Railway closed in 1962, many of its locomotives survive elsewhere. The Llanberis Lake Railway runs on part of the trackbed of the Padarn Railway, while many of the small quarry locomotives were rescued from Dinorwic in the 1969 auction to find new leases of life on tourist railways on both sides of the Atlantic.

The 4ft gauge Padarn Railway ran from the Dinorwic Quarries to Port Dinorwic. The 1ft 11 ½ in gauge slate wagons were carried on transporter wagons behind one of three Hunslet 0-6-0Ts. (I.A. Peden)

The Nantlle Railway remained-horse worked throughout its existence. *Corwen* and *Prince* are at the transhipment yards at Tal-y-Sarn. (Hugh Davies Collection)

The Nantlle Railway was operated like a turnpike road; anyone could use it subject to the regulations prevalent. Payment was made according to the load and distance. (Hugh Davies Collection)

The Penrhyn Quarry Railway ran from the Bethesda Quarry to Port Penrhyn near Bangor and possessed three handsome Hunslet 0-4-0STs. *Linda* is shunting at Port Penrhyn in 1951. (Hugh Davies Collection)

Blanche is at the other end of the line at Bethesda, again in 1951. Both *Linda* and *Blanche* were bought by the Festiniog Railway when the Penrhyn Quarry Railway closed in the early 1960s.

23 May 1961 finds *Linda* at work at Coed-y-Parc on an up train of slate empties. Livery appears to be plain black, a far cry from the splendid fully lined paintwork of earlier years. (M.J. Messenger)

Blanche runs into Coed-y-Parc with a short train of empty wagons. Sufficient trains were worked each day to keep the upper yard at Bethesda clear of loaded wagons. (Hugh Davies Collection)

Port Penrhyn was an interchange yard between the narrow gauge and standard gauge lines. *Blanche* is seen shunting loaded slate wagons, with the standard gauge line coming in at the right. (Hugh Davies Collection)

As the quarries at Bethesda declined so the number of stored 1ft 11 ½ in gauge locomotives increased at Coed-y-Parc. (Hugh Davies Collection)

Above: On Wednesday 13 July 2005 their Royal Highnesses the Prince of Wales and the Duchess of Cornwall visited the Talyllyn Railway to open its new Tywyn Wharf Station and Narrow Gauge Railway Museum building, which replaced the old building seen here. Apart from the new museum the station redevelopment comprises a new kitchen and refreshment room, educational resource room, improved railway shop, stores, guards' room, toilets and office accommodation. Funded by £682,500 from the Heritage Lottery Fund and additional monies from The Wales Tourist Board, the Welsh Development Agency, the Welsh Assembly Government, Gwynedd County Council, the Council for Museums in Wales and donations totalling over £550,000 from members and friends.

Left: Rough Pup is a typical small quarry 0-4-0ST built by Hunslet of Leeds. Still in its original configuration it makes an interesting comparison with those active members of the class at Bala and Llyn Padarn.